# THE EXCAVATION OF MEDIEVAL AND POST-MEDIEVAL REMAINS AT POYLE HOUSE, BERKS, 1999

*by Stuart Foreman, Alan Hardy and Andrew Mayes*

*with contributions by*
*Leigh Allen, Paul Blinkhorn, Bethan Charles, Nick Mitchell,*
*Ruth Pelling, Mark Robinson, Ianto Wain and Hugo Lamdin-Whymark*

Oxford Archaeological Unit
Occasional Paper No 8
May 2001

This book is number eight in a series of Occasional Papers published by the Oxford Archaeological Unit. The series aims to provide a means for the rapid publication and dissemination of short reports for which there is no established provision elsewhere.

ISBN 0 904220 22 2

# CONTENTS

## List of Figures

## List of Tables

*Oxford Archaeological Unit Occasional Paper Number 8*

# THE EXCAVATION OF MEDIEVAL AND POST-MEDIEVAL REMAINS AT POYLE HOUSE, BERKS, 1999

*by Stuart Foreman, Alan Hardy and Andrew Mayes*

*with contributions by*

*Leigh Allen, Paul Blinkhorn, Bethan Charles, Nick Mitchell,*

*Ruth Pelling, Mark Robinson, Ianto Wain and Hugo Lamdin-Whymark*

**SUMMARY**

Archaeological excavations at the site of Poyle House, a derelict Georgian country house, revealed limited evidence of earlier buildings on the site. These comprised the beamslots of a possible farm range, and structural remains of the north wall of a medieval house. The buildings formed part of the medieval Poyle Manor, and limited artefactual evidence suggests that occupation began during the late 11th or 12th centuries. Some evidence for the layout of the house and outbuildings in the Georgian period, and later, was also recorded. Five worked flints were recovered, all residual in later contexts. Pieces present were of Mesolithic and late Neolithic/early Bronze Age date (2000-1700BC).

**PROJECT BACKGROUND**

Planning permission was granted to Gulf Air by Spelthorne District Council (Surrey) in 1994, for the construction of a hotel and car parking on the site of Poyle House, a derelict Georgian country house that had been destroyed by fire in 1969. Following the transfer of Poyle from Surrey to Berkshire, a condition requiring a staged programme of archaeological work was attached to the planning permission by Berkshire County Council. An evaluation undertaken by Oxford Archaeological Unit in October 1999 confirmed the presence of significant medieval deposits on the site (see below). Following on-site discussions with the local authority's archaeological advisor (R. Bourn, Babtie Group) and submission of a Written Scheme of Investigation, a programme of further excavation work was conducted in November and December 1999. The excavation aimed to produce a refined chronological model of the site based on the significant archaeological deposits affected by the development, and to characterise the intensity, status and environment of the settlement from recovered artefactual and ecofactual assemblages. The archaeological data would be augmented by a selective analysis of cartographic and documentary sources.

**Site Location** *(Figure 1)*

The parish of Poyle now falls within Berkshire (Slough Unitary Authority) but has at various times in the past belonged to Middlesex, Surrey and Greater London. The site of Poyle House occupies an area of c 0.5 ha to the west of the village (NGR TQ 0300 7650), on the north bank of a stream known as Poyle Channel, a tributary of the Colne Brook.

**Geology and Topography**

Poyle lies on the floodplain of the Colne Brook, c 5 km north of its confluence with the Thames. The natural geology of the site consists of alluvial silty clay overlying floodplain gravel.

The site has been occupied since the medieval period by Poyle House and its associated buildings and grounds. At the time of excavation the only visible remains of the last house, a mansion originally built around 1700, comprised piles of building debris in the central part of the site, obscured by heavy undergrowth. The surviving stable and service block, converted to residential use, now forms a separate property to the west of the site. A water channel to the west of the site (Fig. 2), once thought to be a medieval moat, has

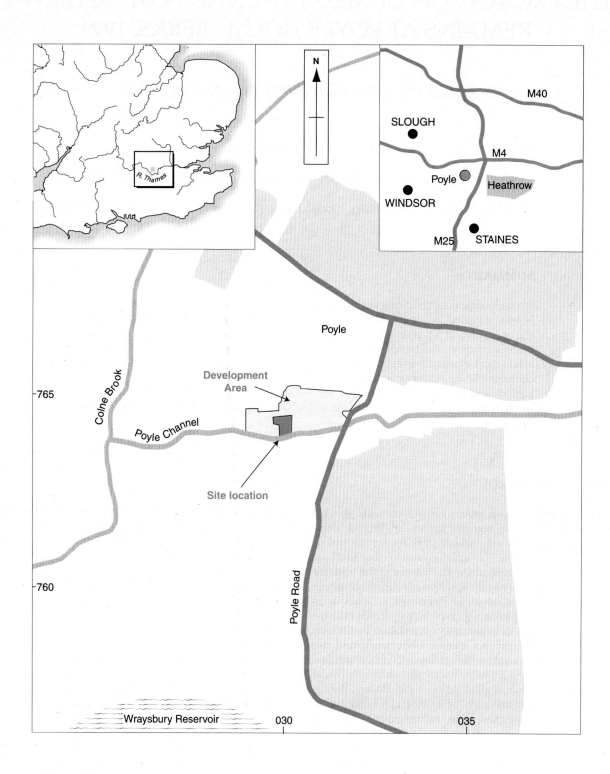

*Figure 1. Site Location.*

subsequently been identified as a probable ornamental garden feature of 19th century origin (RCHME: NMR no. TQ 07 NW1).

## ARCHAEOLOGICAL AND HISTORICAL BACKGROUND
### by Ianto Wain

The site lies in an area noted for evidence of prehistoric activity. Excavations at Stanwell Moor, Yeoveney, and Heathrow have revealed Neolithic enclosures and Bronze Age field systems. Some evidence of Iron Age and Roman farmsteads has been revealed on slightly higher ground to the south-west. Poyle and Horton are mentioned in Domesday and may be Saxon in origin, although no convincing archaeological evidence for Saxon settlement has been recovered in the area.

In the medieval period, the site lay within the medieval parish of Stanwell, part of Spelthorne Hundred in Middlesex. A manor at Stanwell is first mentioned in Domesday, suggesting that there was a settlement here in the years before the Conquest. Poyle itself is not specifically mentioned as a manor, although the Domesday entry for Stanwell suggests that the manor contained two subsidiary estates, one of which may have occupied the site of what later became Poyle Manor. The Domesday entry for Stanwell indicates that the late 11th-century settlement at Stanwell was fairly prosperous: the manor is described as supporting more than 40 households and as containing 4 mills and 3 weirs, which between them produced over 1400 eels per annum.

The documentary sources (VCH Middlesex III, 39-40) suggest that Poyle developed as an independent estate in the early 13th century. It is first mentioned by name in 1235 when it was recorded that Walter de Poyle held land within Stanwell and, although this is not *prima facie* evidence for the existence of the manor at this time, it is perhaps more likely than not that this reference records the existence of some form of settlement. More definite evidence comes from a document of 1265. The Calendar of Inquisitions for this year records that 'William de Poyle held one carucate of land worth 12 marks. William de Bello Campo and John de Purden took and carried off the goods found there'. This reference is of interest not only for the light that it throws upon the political instability of the times (England was embroiled at this time in the so called 'Barons' War' precipitated by Simon de Montfort's rebellion against Henry III and this looting would appear likely to be evidence of this factionalism) but also because it would appear to suggest that by 1265 the estate was both well established and prosperous enough to contain goods worth stealing. Nevertheless the actual landholding is not large (a carucate, more commonly known as a hide, is defined as being sufficient land to support one household for a year). The second half of the 13th century saw consolidation of the holding and by 1299 the manor would appear to have been the centre of a prosperous estate. The Chancery records of this year recorded that the holdings of the manor included a house and a mill, associated with 50 acres of demesne arable land (land held by the lord of the manor for his own use). The estate also included a further 72 acres of arable held by free tenants, suggesting that the manor now contained a small independent settlement away from the area of the house.

The descent of the manor is well documented throughout the medieval period, although the documentary references do not materially enhance our knowledge of the estate. The last useful medieval reference comes from the Chancery Rolls for 1423, and indicates that by this time the estate comprised a house and 200 acres of arable with an additional 40 acres each of pasture and meadow.

Poyle Manor, which appears to have become united with Stanwell Manor sometime in the early 16th century, passed into the ownership of the crown in 1542 and remained crown property until 1612. During this period it was leased to various people including, between 1587 and 1591, the well-known Elizabethan miniaturist painter Nicholas Hilliard. Earlier this century it was claimed that the family of the poet John Milton (1608-1674) leased the manor as a second home outside London, and that Milton spent much of his early life there, although there is no firm evidence to support such a claim. Even after it ceased to be crown property the manor remained united with Stanwell Manor, and when it finally gained its independence in 1678 it appears to have lost its manorial status and henceforward is referred to as Poyle House or Poyle Farm. The estate was enlarged in the 18th century when it occupied most of the land between the western boundary of the parish, the Bath Road to the north, the Wraysbury River and Poyle Road.

The last house was built c 1700, possibly incorporating elements of a Tudor predecessor, although the recorded earlier features, including a brick fireplace in the east wing and elements of the staircase, may have been brought from elsewhere. The south front was constructed in the later 18th century and various additions and alterations were made at later periods. The house was destroyed by fire in 1969.

There are references to a mill within the holdings of the manor in 1299, 1423 and finally in 1612. The precise location of the mill is not specified, but it was probably on the same site as the later village mill which survived into the 20th century, and stood to the east of the manor-house in the village of Poyle. The history of the village mill is well attested (VCH Middlesex III, 42-3). The first secure reference to it as operating independently from the manor comes in 1636 (ibid, 43) and there are numerous further references to it throughout the post-medieval period. It appears to have had a somewhat chequered history, being used variously as a corn mill, paper mill, leather mill and for the making of asbestos and card.

### Summary of the evaluation

The archaeological evaluation carried out by OAU in October 1999 comprised four machine excavated trenches, situated at points over the footprint of the proposed development (see Figure 2). Only Trench 1,

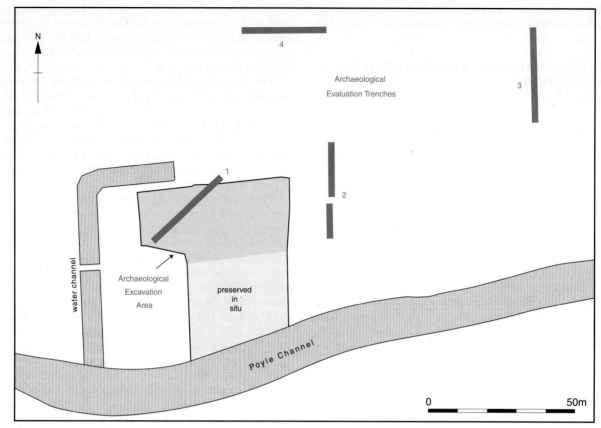

*Figure 2. Location of evaluation trenches and excavation area.*

sited immediately to the west of the footprint of Poyle House, revealed significant archaeological deposits in the form of a number of linear features and pits and an assemblage of 12th- to 13th-century pottery. Trench 2 revealed features and general disturbance relating to buildings associated with the post-medieval Poyle House, but no earlier material. Trenches 3 and 4 revealed no significant archaeology. Following discussions between OAU and the archaeological curator, an excavation area was defined to investigate the remains identified in Trench 1.

**The watching brief**

In the short interval between the end of the excavation fieldwork and the decision to modify the development plans to totally preserve the stratified medieval deposits revealed in the south section (see Figure 2), a precautionary watching brief was maintained on the initial groundworks over the area. No archaeological features or deposits of significance were observed.

**Archaeological description** *(Figure 3 and 4)*

**Excavation methodology**

An area of approximately 1185 sq m, situated within part of the footprint of the proposed buildings was stripped of overburden using a mechanical excavator equipped with a toothless ditching bucket. The overburden averaged 1.1 m in depth. Brick footings of the recently demolished Poyle House were revealed during the removal of the overburden but in most cases, as their position was recorded in section, they were removed to enable a lower horizon of medieval activity to be revealed. In the event the first identifiable horizon in plan was the natural subsoil at approximately 19.2-19.3 m OD, which was significantly lower than that observed in the south section. All exposed archaeological features were manually cleaned, sample excavated and recorded following standard Oxford Archaeological Unit practice (Wilkinson 1992).

**The results**

*General*

The overall depth of overburden clearly indicated episodes of truncation of early deposits and features - by both cultivation and building - and considerable amounts of levelling up with imported material. This effectively removed approximately 0.30 m of medieval archaeology, leaving only the truncated bases of features and no layers within the excavation area. In contrast, the coincidence of the southern edge of the trench with the northern limit of a substantial block of surviving medieval stratigraphy provided ample evidence of medieval development and activity. Following consultations with the curator and the client, it was decided to preserve this area of surviving archaeology in situ.

4

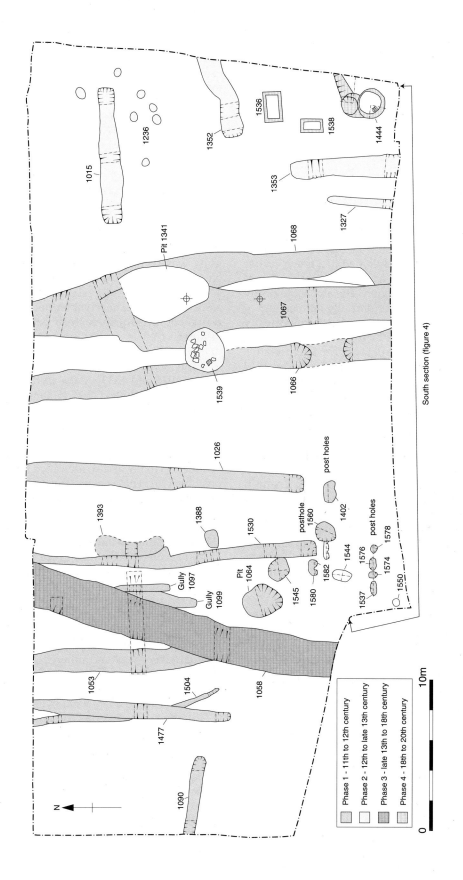

*Figure 3. Plan of archaeological features.*

Nearly all of the pottery recovered in the excavation came from the truncated medieval features, and only a few sherds were recovered from the cleaning of the stratigraphy revealed in the south section. Because of the truncation and disturbance over the excavation area the potential for both residuality and intrusion of dating material is high. The dearth of pottery dated later than the 14th century is almost certainly attributable to the removal of medieval deposits during these episodes of truncation and levelling.

**The Phasing**

The phasing and chronology are based as far as possible on the revealed stratigraphy, augmented by ceramic dating, and for the post-medieval period, historical documentation. The almost complete removal of deposits relating to the period from the 13th century to the 18th century has of necessity led to a much cruder phasing than is suggested by the (mostly undated) stratigraphy in the south section. The archaeologically undatable gap between the ceramically defined end of phase 2 (the late 13th century) and the historically defined beginning of phase 4 (the early 18th century) has been identified simply as phase 3. The interpretative phasing of the south section (shown in Figure 4) should therefore be considered with caution, as it is not possible to define its stratigraphic parameters with any certainty.

*Phase 1: 11th - 12th century (Figure 3 and 4)*

The earliest features were the truncated bases of a group of three N-S ditches (1066, 1067 and 1068). Each was a shallow 'U' shape in profile and averaged c 2.0 m in width and survived to a depth of 0.30 m. They probably represent three phases of a field or property boundary. All three features were filled by a dark grey silty clay which was artefactually sterile apart from a curved piece of worked timber from the fill (1241) of ditch 1067 (see Figure 5 and Mitchell below for a detailed description and analysis of the timber). An environmental sample (no.112 - context 1434) from the fill of ditch 1067 suggested an open, arable environment, with the water table very close to ground level. It would be reasonable to conclude that these ditches would have had stagnant or slow moving water in them for most of the year.

The three ditches appear to be successive definitions of the eastern limit of a concentration of activity. The sequence ran from west to east, with ditch 1066 the earliest, and 1068 the latest.

Two parallel gullies (1026 and 1530) were situated approximately 3.5 m to the west of the earliest boundary ditch 1066. Their profiles, shallow and 'U' shaped, suggest that they may represent the beam slots for a long narrow building, possibly a range set alongside the building defined in the south section (see below). Two pits (1388, 1393) against the east side of beamslot 1530 produced fired clay/daub which is likely to derive from the building's superstructure. Environmental samples were taken from the primary fill of both pits (pit 1393, fill 1394, sample 111; pit 1388, fill 1390, sample 110), and from beamslot 1530 (samples 108 and 113). All four

samples produced numerous remains of charred cereal grain, dominated by bread wheat and hulled barley, with oats, rye and peas present in smaller quantities. Weed seeds were scarce. Sample 108 also showed evidence of later disturbance, probably due to tree planting or animal activity, and contained leaves and buds of ornamental garden trees introduced in the 16th century or later.

Further to the west were five further N-S gullies or shallow ditches (1477,1504, 1053, 1099, and 1097), all filled with a similar grey silty clay. None produced any pottery, although a bone-handled knife (SF1 - see Allen below and Figure 6) was recovered from the fill (1096) of gully 1097 during the evaluation. Also recovered from 1096 were further fragments of fired clay or daub, some showing possible wattle marks. A small assemblage of animal bone was recovered from the excavated parts of the gullies. At the western edge of the site a W-E oriented gully was revealed (1090), extending from under the baulk to a point close to the southern termini of both 1477 and 1504, suggesting a possible functional association. It is conceivable that the evidence could represent the south-eastern corner of a building, although that is at best speculative, and cannot be demonstrated by the surviving archaeological deposits.

Immediately to the south of the termini of beamslot gullies 1026 and 1530 were a scatter of shallow single and double postholes (1580, 1560, 1402, 1578, 1576,1574, and 1537). Two further postholes (1163 and 1167) which by their location and stratigraphic position appear to be associated with this group were identified in the short northern return in the southern section. A possible beamslot (1165) was also identified in section alongside posthole 1167. These postholes may have defined a west-east access way between the buildings to the north and south.

The truncated remains of two large pits (1064 and 1545) were situated immediately to the west of beamslot 1530. The surviving lower fills of 1064 (1065 and 1315) contained an assemblage of 11th- to12th-century pottery. Some (possibly intrusive) 13th-century pottery was recovered from the upper fill (1486) of 1545.

*The south section*
Within the southern section, natural silty clay (1258) in alluvial layers was encountered at a level of 19.63 m OD at the highest point (approximately 0.40 m above the level of undisturbed natural as revealed in plan). These alluvial deposits were overlain by a ploughsoil (1245) which also overlay the undisturbed lower part of the phase 1 boundary ditch 1066, and did not contain any datable material. A deep, flat-bottomed feature (1374) cut the ploughsoil and extended for c 8.80 m along the section, beginning approximately 1.80 m west of ditch 1066. The feature could represent an east-west oriented beamslot for a structure contemporary with the boundary ditches, which was subsequently back filled with a silty clay (1175). Alternatively, and perhaps more likely, cut 1374 and deposit 1175 may represent the construction of a firm building platform. This deposit contained pottery dating to the 12th century.

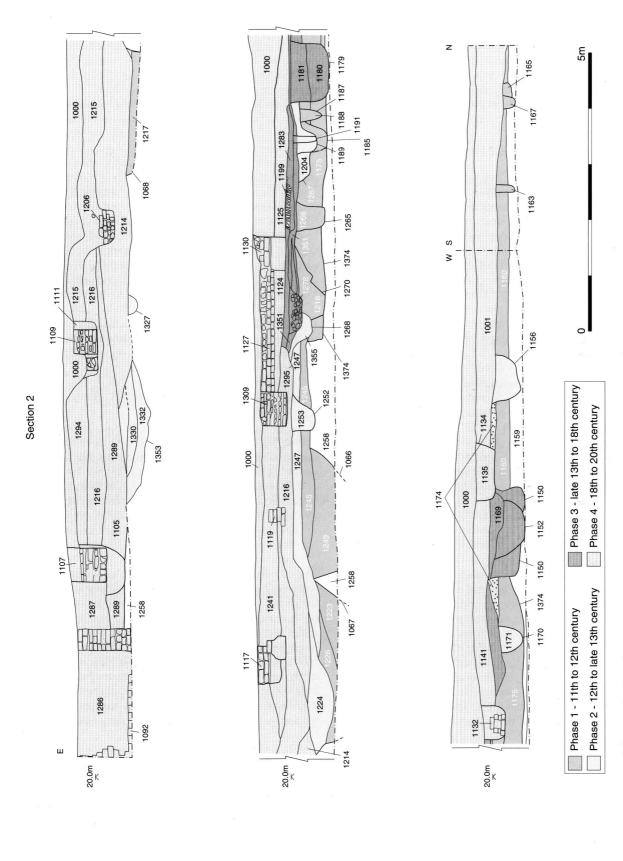

*Figure 4. Section of the south side of excavation area.*

Three large features (1185, 1265 and 1270) representing either postholes or possibly the northern termini of ditches or beamslots, were cut through 1175, at intervals of approximately 1.5 m, to the base of the platform cut 1374. The end of a wooden plank was revealed in the base of 1270. Although the possibility that it was an element of the structure in situ was considered, the modest size of the timber (0.3m x 0.06 m in section) suggests that it is more likely to be a piece of the superstructure discarded in feature 1270 during the demolition. At the west end of the site the natural clay (1159) was overlaid by a ploughsoil (1160).

### Phase 2: 12th -13th century (Figure 3 and 4)

Three truncated shallow gullies (1015, 1352, 1353), one possible slot (1327) and a group of apparently associated postholes (1236) were identified at the east end of the trench. The fills of these features were a fairly similar dark grey silty clay. The features survived to a maximum of 0.45 m in depth and were virtually devoid of finds, with the exception of a small sherd of residual Roman pottery. Their alignment suggests an association with the medieval development to the west, and the postholes (incorporated with or adjacent to the ditches) could indicate a structure, although what form it may have taken cannot be surmised on the strength of the surviving evidence.

A large pit (1539), possibly representing a robbed-out well, was located cutting the boundary ditches 1066 and 1067. Only the top few centimetres of the fill (1540) were investigated. The presence of mortar and brick fragments in the upper fill suggests that any superstructure was levelled when the 18th-century house was constructed. Pottery dating to the 13th century was also found in the upper fill, which might suggest that the feature was backfilled much earlier.

### The south section in phases 2 and 3

An expansion and redevelopment of the site appeared to be indicated by a considerable amount of levelling-up of the eastern part of the site. The phase 1 boundary ditches were sealed by dumped layers of mixed silty clay and redeposited natural clay silt (1247). This covered the two western boundary ditches (1066 and 1067), but possibly left the eastern ditch (1068) open.

A series of three postholes or beamslots were recorded (1189, 1268, and 1252), the former displaying a postpipe (1191), and cutting another posthole (1187) immediately to the west. Feature 1252 was situated approximately 1.4 m to the east of the platform edge defined by phase 1 cut 1374. The fills of these three features were similar, being a mix of silty clay, gravel, and some daub fragments. They probably relate to the structure of the north wall of the building. Two further postholes of similar size (1170 and 1156) were situated further to the west, and both appear to be respected by an intervening floor surface, up to 0.15 m deep, of compacted gravel and small stone (1174). These features are on the same alignment as the beamslots 1530 and 1026 seen in plan, and this might suggest that they represent a contemporary building, to the south.

A series of floor and occupation deposits (1351) stratigraphically overlay the fills of postholes 1189 and 1268, but appeared to respect the postpipe within posthole 1189, thereby suggesting that they represent the same building phase. The floor layers comprised lenses of silty clay and gravel (some of which showed signs of burning) and charcoal rich spreads. A dump of stone rubble (1278) had been laid in a shallow feature (1276), presumably to counter localised subsidence, over the earlier phase 1 posthole 1270..

Set within the uppermost of these lenses (1283) was a hearth (1199) consisting of reddish brown tiles set on edge within a heavily burnt clay matrix. The eastern and western limits of the floor deposits (1351) were truncated by later features. The truncation to the east is assigned to phase 3, and is described below. The western limit of floor 1351 was truncated by a large 'U' shaped feature (1179) measuring 1.1 m wide x 0.70 m deep. The fills (1180 and 1181) were mixes of silty clay, gravel, and brick or tile fragments. The size of the feature could suggest that it represents a robber trench for a masonry or brick wall, although a very substantial beam slot is also a possible explanation. A similar feature (1150) was revealed some 3.2 m to the west, and measured 1.5 m wide x 0.70 m deep, although this could actually represent two, or even three intercutting features. Both features were cut from approximately the same level, and appear to represent the final events of this phase of activity.

### Phase 4: 18th-20th centuries (Figure 3 and 4)

A major redevelopment of the site is indicated by the truncating of the eastern edge of the phase 2 building, recorded in the southern section as cut 1295, and the dumping of deep make up layers (1214, 1216 and 1289) of mixed friable silty clay and gravel with inclusions of brick, tile and stone rubble. The truncating cut was also identified in the northern section (1531), although the infilling material contained considerably less in the way of brick and tile inclusions.

A broad shallow ditch (1058), oriented NNE-SSW and curving slightly to the south, was revealed in the western part of the trench cutting through several of the phase 1 gullies. A considerable amount of brick and tile fragments were recovered from its humic lower fills (1059 and 1093). A quantity of medieval pottery, most likely residual, was also recovered (contexts 1035, 1061, 1094). Analysis of samples of the fill indicated that the ditch may have contained running water (see Robinson below), and suggests that it could have been a late medieval or early post-medieval decorative water feature, infilled during the demolition of the medieval house.

Elements of the Georgian house were recorded in the eastern and southern sections. Three brick lined features, two rectangular (1536,1538) and one circular (1444) were probably soakaways under the service wing of the house. Other brick footings and part of a possible infilled cellar (1092) were located at the south-eastern extremity of the trench. The bricks that comprised these footings are described in detail by Mitchell, below. Some further augmentation of the original groundplan of the house was evident in the brick footing extension (1127) on the west side of the building, the concrete pad (1124) laid down over the phase 2 hearth deposits, and the additional footing (1130).

The west end of the trench showed a fairly homogeneous cultivation soil (1001) overlying the medieval cultivation soil (1160). A short length of brick wall (1526) visible in section in the north-west corner of the trench could represent a garden wall alongside the north edge of the 19th-century ornamental channel, the east-west arm of which was situated just to the north-west of the excavation.

In the northern section two brick footings (1519 and 1292) were noted as probably defining the east and west sides of a separate north-south oriented range.

## ARTEFACTUAL EVIDENCE

### The Pottery
*by Paul Blinkhorn*

*Introduction*

The pottery assemblage comprised 149 sherds with a total weight of 4,268 g. The minimum number of vessels, by measurement of rimsherd length, was 2.97. Three sherds (29 g) were Romano-British, the rest early medieval or later. The pottery occurrence by number and weight of sherds per context by fabric type is shown in Appendix 1.

The assemblage is too small to allow much meaningful analysis beyond provenance and chronology, but nevertheless appears typical of contemporary domestic sites in the region.

*Fabrics*

A significant proportion of the medieval pottery from the site, particularly the earlier wares, are the same types as those in use in the City of London at that time. Consequently, the equivalent Museum of London Archaeological Service (MoLAS) pottery fabric codes and chronologies have been used where appropriate (Vince, 1985).

*Early Surrey Ware (ESUR) 1050-1150.*
*11 sherds, 173 g, MNV = 0.19*

*Early Medieval Shelly Ware (EMSH) 11th-12th century.*
23 sherds, 489 g, MNV = 0

*London-type Ware (LOND) Early 12th-late 14th century.*
*1 sherd, 3 g, MNV = 0*

*South Hertfordshire Grey Ware (SHER) 12th-14th century.*
*25 sherds, 874 g, MNV = 0.77.*

*Coarse Border Ware (CBW) Late 13th century-c 1500.*
*6 sherds, 246 g, MNV = 0.50*

*Tudor Green Ware (TUDG) c AD1380-1500.*
*1 sherd, 5 g, MNV = 0*

The following wares were also noted:

*Brill/Boarstall Ware. c.AD1200-?1600 (Mellor 1994).*
Wheel-thrown. Hard buff, orange, pale pink, or yellow-grey fabric, sometimes with fine 'pimply' surface. Rare to common sub-angular to sub-rounded orange, clear and grey quartzite up to 0.5mm, rare subrounded to sub-angular red ironstone up to 1mm. Mottled pale to dark glossy green exterior glaze, often with copper filings. Applied rouletted strips common, sometimes in red-firing clay; rosettes, spirals also occur. Usually 'three-decker' or baluster jugs, although puzzle jugs also known. Jars, bowls, etc occur at end of medieval period. Later vessels plainer, and include the full range of medieval and early post-medieval vessel types.
1 sherd, 71 g, MNV = 0.

*Medieval Fine Sandy Ware I. c.12th-14th century.*
Abundant sub-angular quartz up to 0.5 mm. Handmade and wheel-thrown vessels. A range of these fine, grey sandy wares from several different sources were in use throughout the south midlands during the medieval period (Mellor 1994).
17 sherds, 1,146 g, MNV = 0.66.

*Medieval Sandy Ware II. 11/12th century?*
Moderate to dense sub-rounded, clear, black and red quartz up to 1 mm. Rare angular white flint and silver mica. Undistinctive ware with numerous parallels throughout southern England.
9 sherds, 153 g, MNV = 0.

*'M40' Ware: 12th century (Hinton 1974).*
Hard, flint and limestone unglazed ware, with a known kiln source at Camley Gardens near Maidenhead (Pike 1965). Known at numerous sites in south Oxfordshire and Berkshire. Some vessels have distinctive vertical combing on the body.
43 sherds, 811 g, MNV = 0.77.

*Cistercian Ware: c.AD1470-1550 (McCarthy and Brooks 1988).*
Hard, smooth fabric, usually brick-red, but can be paler or browner. Few visible inclusions, except for occasional quartz grains. Range of vessel forms somewhat specialised, and usually very thin-walled (c 2 mm). Rare white slip decoration.
1 sherd, 6 g.

*Red Earthenwares:*
Fine sandy earthenware, usually with a brown or green glaze, occurring in a range of utilitarian forms. Such 'country pottery' was first made in the 16th century, and in some areas continued in use until the 19th century (McCarthy and Brooks 1988).
2 sherds, 76 g, MNV = 0.

## Chronology

The range of fabric and vessel forms suggests that the main period of occupation in the excavated area was during the 11th to 13th centuries, with little activity thereafter. It should be emphasised, however that the paucity of late medieval and post-medieval material has almost certainly been exaggerated by episodes of landscaping.

It is possible, on basis of the chronology of the major wares, to produce a series of phases, as shown in Table 1.

*Table 1. Pottery Phasing, defining wares.*

| Phase | Date | Defining Wares |
|---|---|---|
| 1 | 11th - 12th Century | EMSH, ESUR |
| 2 | 12th - Late 13th Century | M40, SHER |
| 3 | Late 13th/14th Century | CBW, Brill |

It is possible that the contexts dated to the 11th century may simply be later deposits which do not have contemporary pottery, as most only produced a few sherds.

Very little post-13th-century pottery was noted. A single context produced a Brill/Boarstall bottle base, a vessel type which is generally 14th-century or later, although examples have been dated to the later 13th century (Mellor 1994, fig. 55). Coarse Border Ware first came into use c 1270 in London, although it did not generally occur until post-1300, and did not become common until around the middle of the 14th century (N Jeffries, pers. comm.), so the late 13th-century start-date for phase 3 should be very much regarded as a terminus post quem. A single context (1415) is datable to the 16th century, and a sherd of Cistercian ware (late 15th-16th century) was noted during the evaluation (context 114).

The pottery occurrence per site phase was as shown in Table 2.

*Table 2. Pottery occurence by number and weight of sherds (in g) and minimum number of vessels (MNV).*

| Phase | Number of Sherds | Weight (g) | MNV |
|---|---|---|---|
| 1 | 14 | 229 | 0.09 |
| 2 | 114 | 3181 | 2.24 |
| 3 | 15 | 743 | 0.64 |
| Total | 358 | 3924.09 | 2.97 |

## Vessel use

The data in Table 3 show a typical pattern for domestic sites of the early medieval period. Jars are by far the commonest vessel type during the early phase, along with a small number of bowls, with jugs rapidly coming to dominate the assemblage by the later 13th century.

Tablewares, which became increasing common from the 14th century onwards, are not represented except

by the single bottle sherd from a phase 3 context. This could suggest a hiatus in activity from around the mid-late 14th century, although as is stated above, later landscaping has probably had a major effect on the assemblage size. Other than the fact that the assemblage is typical of domestic sites of the period, no assessment of the site status can be made from the pottery.

*Table 3. Vessel use per phase, expressed as a percentage of the minimum number of vessels per phase.*

| Phase | Jars | Bowls | Jugs | Other | Total MNV |
|---|---|---|---|---|---|
| 1 | 100% | 0% | 0% | 0% | 0.09 |
| 2 | 77.2% | 11.6% | 11.2% | 0% | 2.24 |
| 3 | 21.9% | 0% | 78.1% | Bottle* | 0.64 |
| Total MNV | 1991 | 0.116 | 0.893 | 0% | 2.97 |

*Diagnostic vessel represent by non-rim sherds

## The waterlogged wood
*by Nick Mitchell*

Three fragments of worked wood were recovered from deposits on the site. A short, broad post was recovered from posthole 1560. It is oak heartwood and has been radially split with all four faces axed to a broad point. It most likely represents the discarded base of a structural post.

A part-circular oak plank, 0.42 x 0.15 x 0.025m, was found in the fill of beamslot 1026 and is probably part of a barrel lid or base. The smaller straight side is badly rotted and may not reflect the true edge. The long side has the appearance of a rebate cut to fit the adjoining plank but this coincides exactly with the transition from heartwood to sapwood. The sapwood has suffered severe shrinkage and the original form of this edge cannot be known. Two circular holes have been drilled in the plank and may be punctures for releasing the contents of the barrel. However, it would be unusual to find two such holes so close to each other and it is possible that at least one could be for securing a batten pegged across this barrel lid or base to join the constituent planks. This plank is made from very straight-grained, slow-grown oak and may not derive from this country.

### The oak wheel felloe (Figure 5)

Part of an oak wheel was sealed by 13th-century deposits in phase 1 ditch 1067. The felloe is almost complete and survives to a length of 1.26m. It is 0.115m broad (across its working surface) and 0.1m thick with the external diameter calculated to have been approximately 2.1m. The ends of the felloe are stop-splayed face-halved scarf joints, both of which are damaged but appear to have been secured to the neighbouring felloes with just two pegs per joint, although the joints do not survive intact. There is a single shallow lap-joint, which appears not to have been cut perfectly orientated to the centre of the wheel. It is therefore possible that it could have been secured to an axle shaft by means of a clasp-arm construction, which surrounds the axle shaft instead of penetrating it in the style of radial spokes. However, radial spokes seem the most likely form since clasp-arm construction is considered to be a later development (Reynolds 1985, 61-5). It has a single wedged peg made of beech (*Fagus sylvatica*) to secure the spoke which may have been simply lapped over the felloe or trenched across it for added strength. The joint is cut only 16 mm deep to prevent the wheel being weakened, and the inner surface of the timber swells at this point to provide extra bulk to counter the weakening effect of the incision. The grain of the wood is curved to the shape of the wheel and this timber would have been carefully selected to avoid cutting across the grain and weakening the wheel.

A total of seven cog-holes are located at intervals around the rim. The cog-holes are irregularly spaced, with the intervals on the external face from the centre of one hole to the next varying between 155 and 215 mm. The paths of the holes, and thus the cogs, are not radially set but are inclined at varying degrees. The size of the stave-holes is regular at 43 mm diameter but the shapes vary from round to sub-square and may have resulted from prolonged use with a single direction of force applied. There is a circular depression with a rounded base, 12 mm deep and 30 mm across, which

perhaps represents an aborted cog-hole. One of the cog-holes has a second hole drilled partially over it. It penetrates the full breadth of the felloe and has an oak wedge still in place, presumably to tighten the hold on a loose cog.

Three possible interpretations have been considered for the function of this wheel. Some characteristics of the object are similar to those of mill gearwheels, and it may represent one of only a small group of known examples from medieval Britain. The Poyle wheel differs from the gearwheels found at Reading in Berkshire, also sealed by 13th-century deposits, and from the 14th-century wheel known from Chingley Forge, Kent (Crossley 1975, 15), and the 14th-century trip-wheel from Bordesley Abbey, Worcestershire (Allen 1993, 216), which were designed to hold cogs set parallel to their axles. With cogs projecting out from the outer surface of the wheel, the Poyle Manor gear is likely to have driven, or been driven by, a similar gearwheel set at right-angles to it; therefore it could have been mounted either vertically or horizontally.

The inclined angling of the cogs is also seen in the gearwheel from St. Giles' Mill in Reading (Mitchell forthcoming) and may have encouraged the cogs of separate gears to engage. However, the peg-holes of the Poyle Manor gear are set at differing angles and the greatly varying distances between them is a surprising aspect which would presumably prohibit the smooth meshing of one gear to the next. Furthermore, although the diameter of the original wheel is a reasonable size, the robustness of the felloe itself falls well short of what one would expect of a millwheel.

This lends weight to an alternative possibility, that the object is not a gearwheel but a small and early form of water wheel, perhaps of the type illustrated from Hemington Fields in Leicestershire (Salisbury 1995, 34).

A third possibility (and arguably the most attractive on the basis of the evidence surviving) is that it represents part of the rim of a windlass (S. Naylor pers. comm.); the vertical wheel would have turned on a horizontal axle, and the 'cogs' would have provided handholds - there would be no necessity to space them at exact points around the rim. The windlass could have been routinely in use in the farmyard (raising or lowering material to an upper storey of the barn, or raising water from the nearby well) or it could have been used in building operations. Such lightweight mechanical lifting devices appear frequently in medieval illustrations (for instance the drawing of masons building St Albans Abbey from *The Lives of the two Offas*. MS. Cotton Nero D.1 fol. 23v. British Museum); their rare survival in the archaeological record is unsurprising given the material from which they were made.

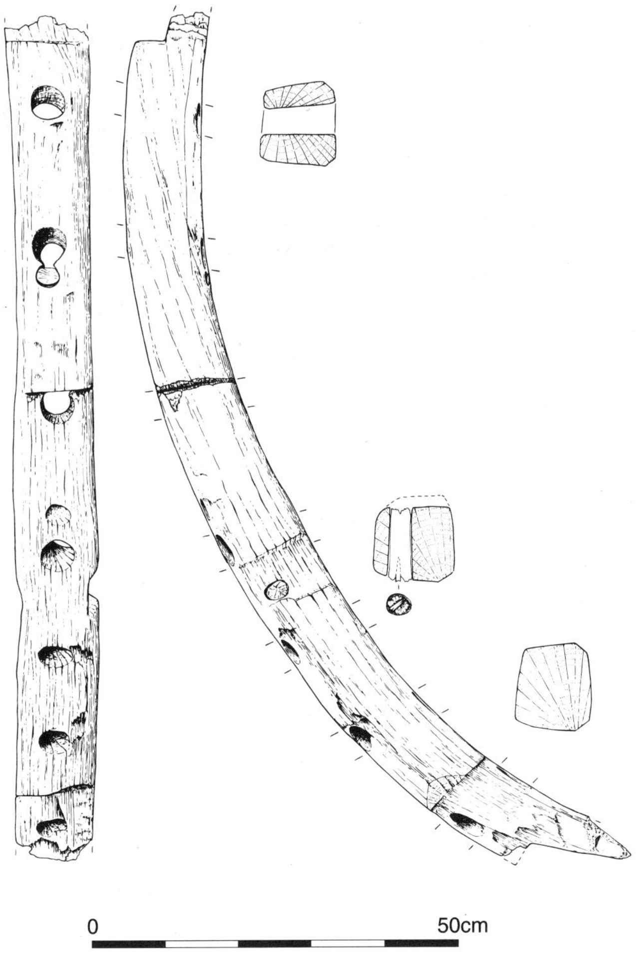

0                          50cm

*Figure 5. Curved oak felloe.*

## Building material
*by Nick Mitchell*

A total of 215 fragments of ceramic building material, weighing 27,920 g, was recovered from the excavations. This comprises mostly flat roof tiles and brick with a few curved tiles, two floor bricks and a floor tile. Three bricks are of a thickness that suggests their use in pre-18th-century buildings but most of the material is likely to relate to the Georgian house or to its later additions.

There are 54 brick fragments (4860 g) which were retrieved from 12 different contexts. Thirty-nine of the brick fragments, 520 g, and 6 flat roof tile fragments, 460 g, come from phases 1 or 2. The brick from these contexts consists solely of very small fragments with no diagnostically early features and all the ceramic building material from these phases is likely to be residual.

Most of the material is from phase 3 or 3/4 or phase 4 contexts. Most of this is undiagnostic but there are 11 bricks with a measurable thickness, ranging from 46-68 mm, which can provide a general indication of date. There are three bricks, from contexts 1029, 1034 and 1035, which are less than 54 mm thick and are therefore likely to be pre-18th century in date (Smith 1998, 34) and may have been used in buildings of the medieval manor. Three other hand-made bricks, from contexts 1034, 1035 and 1045 are between 58 and 60 mm thick and these are likely to date to the 18th or 19th century.

The only four complete bricks present were removed from their in situ position in the possible infilled cellar 1092 at the south-eastern limit of the excavation. Two bricks from the floor of this structure are paving bricks with a considerable degree of wear and measure 223 x 82 x 59mm. Two other bricks were taken from the cellar wall, one in a yellow fabric, the other red, and have the same dimensions, 230 x 110 x 65 mm and well-made frogs in one bedding-face only. These frogged bricks are likely to date to the late 18th or 19th century (Brunskill 1990, 24).

There are 153 roof tile fragments weighing 12,640 g. The great majority of this is flat tile although there are three curved pieces from contexts 1045 and 1415, which are probably plain ridge tiles. There are four fabrics used for the roof tile although the assemblage is dominated by two fabrics, one which is high-fired and marked by a swirling marl patterning, and the second which is a soft grog-tempered orange fabric. It is not possible to provide a date range for the use of these tiles as all four fabrics occurred in each phase. No stone roofing material was found and the tiles are likely to reflect the consistent use of ceramic roofing material across phases 3 and 4.

A single well-worn floor tile (180 g) was found in phase 2/3 context 1315. It is 22 mm thick but with no keying on its base and, with any traces of decoration or glaze having been worn away, it is only possible to date this as late medieval at the earliest.

## The metal objects
*by Leigh Allen*

### Introduction

There were 7 iron objects recovered from the site, the most notable among them being a large iron scale-tang knife (SF 1) from evaluation context 111 (Figure 6). The knife is complete although the blade is very corroded. The slightly flaring tang still has the polished bone scales attached by three iron rivets. There are traces of copper alloy on the end of the handle that may represent the remains of an end plate. The blade has a straight back in line with the top of the handle and the blade dips near the tip to meet the blade edge. Scale-tang knives were introduced in the 13th-14th centuries and continued in use into the post-medieval period.

The remaining objects comprise 4 nails from contexts 1047, 1070, 1357 and 1396, a miscellaneous fragment from context 1400 and an iron object from context 1083. The nails are all very corroded and their head types are not identifiable. The iron object (SF1004) is in very poor condition; it is a curved strip with the ends obscured by corrosion and is possibly another nail.

### The catalogue

*Knife, iron, complete.*
Scale-tang knife with a very badly corroded blade and bone scales. There are three iron rivets securing the scales to the tang. There are traces of copper alloy on the end of the handle, which indicates that the knife originally had a copper alloy end plate. The blade appears to have a straight back in line with the top of the handle; the blade dips near the tip to meet the blade edge. L:268mm. Context 111, SF 1.

*Nail, iron, incomplete.*
A nail with a square sectioned shank and a damaged head. L:61mm. Context 1357, SF 1007.

*Nail, iron, incomplete.*
A nail with a square sectioned shank and a damaged head. L:51mm. Context 1047.

*Nail, iron, complete.*
A large nail with a square sectioned head and a flat head. L:107mm. Context 1070, SF 1005.

*Strip/nail, iron, incomplete.*
A strip with a sub-circular section, tapering to a point along its length, probably a fragment from a nail shank. L:36mm. Context 1396.

*Miscellaneous, iron, incomplete.*
Three irregularly shaped fragments of iron. L:17mm, Context 1400, SF 1008.

*Object, iron, incomplete.*
Strip in very poor condition; the ends are obscured by corrosion. L:95mm. Context 1083, SF 1004.

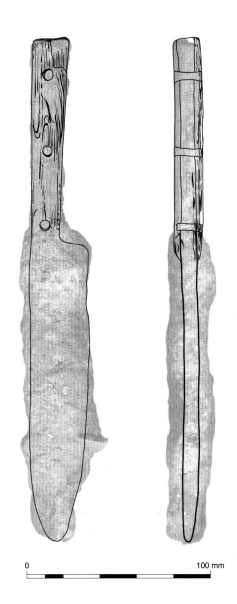

0                                    100 mm

*Figure 6. Bone handled knife (SF1).*

## Worked flint
*by Hugo Lamdin-Whymark*

A total of five flints and 33 (1.389 kg) pieces of burnt unworked flint were recovered from the excavation. The flintwork is all residual, present in the fills of later features. An iron-stained soft hammer struck blade from context 1007 (SF1000) exhibited numerous dorsal blade removals and is probably Mesolithic in date. A thumbnail scraper from context 1305 was manufactured on a hard hammer percussion flake and exhibited relatively fine retouch around the left-hand side and distal; the edge angle was relatively low at 45°. This artefact is late Neolithic/early Bronze Age in date (2500-1700BC). The other flint in the assemblage consisted of a crude broken scraper on a thermally fractured flake, a piece of irregular waste and tested nodule of gravel flint with two flakes removed.

## ECOFACTUAL EVIDENCE

### Animal bones
*by Bethan Charles*

#### Introduction

A total of 130 fragments of bone were retrieved by hand from the site. The vast majority of the bone was recovered from contexts dated from the 12th to 13th century as shown in Table 4.

#### Methodology

Table 4 details the number of identified fragments of bone for each species (NISP). All fragments of bone were counted including elements from the vertebral centrum, ribs and long bone shafts. An attempt was made to separate the sheep and goat bones using the criteria of Boessneck (1969), and Prummel and Frisch (1986). However, since no identifiable goat bones were present in the assemblage all caprine bones are listed as sheep. The ageing of the domestic animals for the assessment was based on tooth eruption and epiphyseal fusion of the bone (all detailed ageing data can be found in the archive). Tooth eruption and wear was measured using Payne's (1973) tables for sheep and Silver's (1969) tables were used to give timing of epiphyseal closure for cattle and sheep. The measurements taken are those defined by von den Driesch (1976) and are detailed in Appendix 2. In all cases the species assemblages are too small to be considered reliable indicators of the relative importance of particular species.

#### Condition

The condition of the bone was measured by grading it from 1 to 5 using the criteria stipulated by Lyman (1996), grade 1 being the best preserved bone and grade 5 indicating that the bone had suffered such structural and attritional damage as to make it unrecognisable. The majority of bone was in good condition with only a few fragments with severe attritional damage. However, it can be seen in Table 5 that many of the bones had recent breaks. A number of the bones displayed gnaw marks likely to have been caused by dogs. Only a few of the bones had been burnt.

A number of the bones displayed butchery marks, mostly consisting of chop marks on the long bone fragments.

#### Species representation

*11th -12th century*
Only ten fragments of bone were identified from this period including long bone fragments from cattle, sheep, domestic fowl, cat and the right radius and ulna of a horse. It is likely that the cattle and sheep represent the main domestic species of the site, although the assemblage was too small to be confidently considered representative.

*Table 4. Number of fragments of identified species by period.*

| Phase | Horse | Cattle | Sheep | Pig | Dog | Cat | D. Goose | D. Fowl | Duck | Unidentified | Total |
|---|---|---|---|---|---|---|---|---|---|---|---|
| 1 | 2** | 3 | 2 | 0 | 0 | 1 | 1 | 0 | 0 | 1 | 10 |
| 2 | 4 | 36 | 8 | 8 | 16* | 0 | 1 | 1 | 1 | 36 | 111 |
| 3 | 0 | 0 | 0 | 0 | 0 | 0 | 0 | 0 | 0 | 1 | 1 |
| Unphased | 0 | 6 | 0 | 0 | 0 | 0 | 0 | 0 | 0 | 2 | 8 |
| Total | 6 | 45 | 10 | 8 | 16 | 1 | 2 | 1 | 1 | 40 | 130 |

** Radius and Ulna *15 of the fragments are from a partial dog skeleton (1394)

*Table 5. Condition of bones according to period.*

| Phase | Butchery | | Burnt | | Gnaw Marks | | Fresh Break | |
|---|---|---|---|---|---|---|---|---|
| | Number | % of total | Number | % of total | Number | % of total | Number | % of total |
| 1 | 3 | 30 | 0 | 0 | 1 | 10 | 2 | 20 |
| 2 | 34 | 31 | 2 | 2 | 11 | 10 | 26 | 23 |
| Unphased | 3 | 38 | 3 | 38 | 0 | 0 | 4 | 38 |
| Total | 40 | | 5 | | 12 | | 32 | |

### 12th -13th century

Cattle dominate the assemblage from this period, with almost half the identified fragments of bone. The small amount of ageing data from bone fusion indicates that the majority of the cattle were over the ages of two to three years old, although Table 6 indicates that at least some of the cattle were being killed at a young age. Part of a cattle skull with its jaw was found in the fill (1054) of ditch terminus 1053. The tooth wear stage indicated that it was killed at around the age of 8-18 months of age. Equal numbers of sheep and pig bones occur in the assemblage. Four horse bones were found from contexts 1025, 1093 and 1566 (the fills of features 1026, 1058 and 1530 respectively). All the bones were long bones and appeared to be from animals over the age of 2 years.

*Table 6. Tooth wear stages.*

| Species | Cattle | Sheep | |
|---|---|---|---|
| Phase | 2 | 1 | 2 |
| | | | |
| 8-18 months | 1 | 0 | 0 |
| 1-2 years | 0 | 1 | 0 |
| 4-6 years | 0 | 0 | 1 |

### Other bones

Part of a dog skeleton was found in pit 1393 (context 1394). It included both femurs and innominate bones as well as the sacrum, all the lumbar vertebrae, one thoracic vertebrae and three fragmented ribs. Ageing the animal from the epiphyseal fusion of the remaining bones produced a figure of around 1.5 years of age at death. However, signs of eburnation on the distal articulations of the femurs could suggest that the animal may have been much older. In addition to this, a single dog ulna was found in context 1057.

Three domestic fowl bones were also identified from Phase 1 and 2 deposits, and the distal half of a cat tibia was found in Phase 1 gully 1090.

### Conclusion

The bones from this site represent a small assemblage, the vast majority of which are from the 12th- to 13th-century deposits. The variety of animal bone including domestic fowl, domestic goose and duck, may be indicative of a mid- to high-status site. The small size of the sample prohibits detailed analysis. However, the assemblage does not appear typical of concentrated butchery waste since there were no high concentrations of animal bones at any part of the site. It is likely that small-scale butchery was taking place as necessary, and it is likely that this assemblage represents both butchery and domestic waste.

A few horse bones were found at the site. The majority of the bones were complete and were likely to be from mature animals. One of the bones displayed gnaw marks, possibly indicating that horsemeat was being fed to the dogs. Cats and dogs were present on the site during the medieval period, probably as working animals as well as pets.

### The charred and waterlogged plant remains
*by Ruth Pelling*

### Introduction

A series of samples were taken from waterlogged ditch/ beamslot and pit deposits in order to recover a representative range of environmental evidence, sufficient to help characterise the medieval occupation. Five samples producing waterlogged material were consequently analysed: sample <112> from a 12th-century ditch fill (cxt 1434), <111> from a 13th-century pit fill (1394), and samples <108> and <113> from a probable 12th- to 13th- century ditch/beamslot (cxts 1337 and 1481). The fifth sample <107> (context 1093) was taken from a possibllate medieval or early post-medieval 18th-century garden feature (1058) that cut across a number of the medieval beamslots and ditches.

In addition sample <110> from pit fill 1390, which produced a large quantity of charred remains, was also analysed.

*Methodology*

Samples of 5 kg or 5 litres were processed by bulk flotation and the flots collected onto a 250μm mesh. Flots were kept wet with the exception of sample 110, which was allowed to air dry once it was established it contained charred remains only. The waterlogged flots were washed through a stack of sieves ranging from 500μm to 2mm. Each fraction was examined under a binocular microscope at x10 to x20 magnification. Any charred remains were extracted and allowed to dry. Insect fragments and quantifiable waterlogged plant fragments or seeds were extracted and kept wet. Identifications of plant remains were based on morphological criteria and by comparison with modern reference material held in the Oxford University Museum. Absolute counts were not made but relative abundance was recorded on a three point scale (+ = present; ++ = common; +++ = abundant). The charred remains, including sample 110, were carefully scanned under the microscope at x10 to x20 magnification once dry. Any seeds and chaff noted were identified and abundance was estimated. Taxonomic order follows Clapham, Tutin and Moore (1989).

*Results*

All five samples examined for waterlogged remains produced a good and varied set of results (see Table 7, below). Charred remains were abundant in three samples (108, 110 and 111 - see Table 8 below). Sample 112 (context 1434) is from an early ditch (1067), interpreted as a field boundary. The sample was dominated by ruderal/arable species including *Brassica rapa* subsp. *sylvestris* (wild turnip), *Polygonum aviculare* (knotgrass), *Stellaria media* agg. (chickweed), *Chenopodium album* (Fat Hen), *Urtica urens* (small nettle) and *U. dioica* (stinging nettle). All these species could simply have been growing on nitrogen rich soil within the settlement although they could equally have occurred as arable weeds. Two further species are more particularly associated with arable crops rather than ruderal habitats. *Anthemis cotula* (stinking mayweed) is very much a weed of cereal crops, while *Thlaspi arvense* (field penny cress) is strongly associated with flax. In addition this sample also contained fragments of legume pod thought to derive from a cultivated bean, vetch or pea.

Frequent seeds of *Lemna sp.* (duckweed) suggest the presence of stagnant water. A number of species are likely to have been growing on the edge of the ditch. This group includes *Sparganium erectum* (branched bur-reed), *Eleocharis palustris* (common spike rush), *Carex sp.* (sedges), *Rumex conglomeratus* (sharp dock), and *Salix sp.* (willow). *Eleocharis palustris* require at least seasonal flooding while *Sparganium erectum* requires the watertable to remain less than 10 cm below the surface. As neither species will tolerate shaded conditions or

running water they would be expected to occur within the margins of the ditch, with their roots under the water. *Picris hieracioides* (hawkweed ox-tongue) and *Medicago lupulina* (black medick) suggest drier grassland conditions, while *Brassica rapa* subsp. *sylvestris* might suggest steep eroding banksides to the ditch.

Samples 111 and 110 are derived from the primary fills of phase 1 pits 1388 and 1393 respectively, and may be associated with a medieval building defined by heavily truncated beamslots. Both samples produced rich deposits of charred remains. Sample 111 also contained waterlogged material consisting largely of species characteristic of the wet ground adjacent to streams or ditches and of arable/ruderal species. Open stagnant water is suggested by seeds of *Lemna sp.*, while *Ranunculus sceleratus* (celery leaved buttercup) may have been growing within the mineral rich water of the pit or wet soils surrounding it. *Eleocharis palustris, Carex sp.* and *Juncus sp.* (sedges) further suggest the presence of wet or marshy ground. The arable/ruderal species include both those characterisitc of ruderal, settlement habitats such as *Aethusa cynapium* (fool's parsley), *Stellaria media, Chenopodium album* and *Lapsana communis* (nipplewort), and two species more characteristic of cereal crops, *Anthemis cotula* and *Valerianella dentata* (narrow-fruited cornsalad).

Charred remains were numerous in both samples 110 and 111, with over 600 items in 5 kg of deposit from sample 110. Free-threshing *Triticum sp.* (wheat) and *Hordeum vulgare* were present in both samples with the *Triticum sp.* slightly more numerous in 110, while sample 111 is conversely dominated by *Hordeum vulgare*. The presence of a hexaploid *Triticum aestivum* (bread wheat) type wheat is confirmed by well preserved rachis. A hulled variety of barley is represented. *Secale cereale* (rye) was rare but was noted in sample 111. *Avena sp.* (oats) were present in both samples and *Vicia/Pisum sp.* (beans/peas etc.) were also present in low numbers. Chaff was a minor element in 110 in relation to grain but was much more prevalent in 111, which produced several rachis of *Secale cereale/Hordeum vulgare* and *H. vulgare*. Weeds were rare in proportion to the cereal grain in both samples and were mostly large seeded. Sample 110 is therefore interpreted as consisting largely of processed grain of wheat and barley with occasional oats, within which only occasional and mostly cereal sized weed seeds remain. Sample 111 is largely a deposit of barley, probably including whole ears retaining the rachis, but cleaned of most of the weeds.

Samples 108 and 113 were taken from phase 1 beamslot 1530, of 12th- to13th-century date, probably relating to a farm building. Sample 108 produced a good deposit of charred remains while occasional charred items were also present in 113. All three deposits, including sample 107, which came from a much later feature, produced good waterlogged remains. The frequent seeds of *Lemna sp.* in 107 and 113 and of *Myriophyllum sp.* (water milfoil) in 107, indicate open stagnant water. *Apium nodiflorum* (fools watercress) in 107 and *Ranunculus sceleratus* in 113 were probably also growing in the muddy waters of the ditches. *Alnus glutinosa* (alder), *Sparganium erectum, Salix sp.* and *Carex*

Table 7. The waterlogged plant remains

| Latin/Scientific name | Common name | | Sample | 107 | 108 | 111 | 112 | 113 |
|---|---|---|---|---|---|---|---|---|
| | | | Context | 1093 | 1337 | 1394 | 1434 | 1481 |
| | | | Feature | 1053 | 1336 | 1393 | 1433 | 1485 |
| | | | Phase | 4 | 1 | 3 | 1 | 1 |
| | | | Volume | 5 l | 5 kg | 5 l | 5 l | 5 kg |
| Ranunculus acris/repens/bulbosus | Buttercup | seed | | - | - | + | - | - |
| Ranunculus subgen Ranunculus | Buttercup | seed | | + | - | - | + | - |
| Ranunculus acris | Meadow Buttercup | seed | | - | + | - | - | - |
| Ranunculus bulbosus | Bulbous Buttercup | seed | | - | + | - | - | + |
| Ranunculus sardous | Hairy Buttercup | seed | | - | + | - | - | - |
| Ranunculus sceleratus | Celery-leaved Buttercup | seed | | - | ++ | ++ | - | +++ |
| Brassica rapa subsp. Sylvestris | Wild Turnip | seed | | - | ++ | - | + | + |
| Thlaspi arvense | Field Penny-Cress | seed | | - | - | - | + | - |
| Silene sp. | Campion/Catchfly | seed | | - | + | - | - | + |
| Silene dioica | Red Campion | seed | | - | - | - | - | + |
| Silene cf. Vulgaris | Bladder/Sea Campion | seed | | - | + | - | - | - |
| Stellaria media agg. | Chickweed | seed | | - | + | + | + | - |
| Chenopodium murale | Nettle-leaved Goosefoot | seed | | - | + | - | - | + |
| Chenopodium album | Fat Hen | seed | | - | ++ | + | + | ++ |
| Atriplex sp. | Orache | seed | | - | ++ | - | - | - |
| Aceraceae/Vitaceae type | Maple/ Virginia Creeper | leaf | | - | + | - | - | - |
| Vicia/Pisum sp. | Vetch/Pea | pod frag | | - | - | - | + | - |
| Medicago lupulina | Black Medick seed pod | pod | | - | - | - | + | - |
| Rosaceae | | thorn | | - | - | - | - | + |
| cf. Pomoideae | Apple/Pear/Hawthorn etc | wood | | + | - | - | - | - |
| Rubus fruticosus | Blackberry/Bramble | seed | | + | + | - | + | + |
| Potentilla sp. | Cinquefoil | seed | | + | - | - | - | - |
| Potentilla anserina | Silverweed | seed | | - | + | - | - | - |
| Potentilla cf. Erecta | Tormentil | seed | | + | - | - | - | - |
| Crataegus sp. | Hawthorn | seed | | - | + | - | - | - |
| Sorbus aria | White beam | leaf | | - | + | - | - | - |
| Myriophyllum sp. | Water-milfoil | seed | | + | - | - | - | - |
| Aethusa cynapium | Fool's Parsley | seed | | - | + | + | - | - |
| Conium maculatum | Hemlock | seed | | - | + | + | + | + |
| Apium nodiflorum | Fool's Watercress | seed | | ++ | - | - | - | - |
| Pastinaca sativa | Wild Parsnip | seed | | + | - | - | - | - |
| Polygonum aviculare | Knotgrass | seed | | + | - | - | + | + |
| Polygonum persicaria/lapathifolium | Redshank/Persicaria | seed | | - | + | + | + | + |
| Fallopia convolvulus | Black Bindweed | seed | | - | + | - | - | + |
| Rumex sp. | Docks | seed | | - | - | - | + | - |
| Rumex conglomeratus | Sharp Dock | seed | | - | - | - | + | - |
| Urtica urens | Small Nettle | seed | | - | + | - | + | ++ |
| Urtica dioica | Common Nettle | seed | | +++ | ++ | ++ | ++ | +++ |
| Alnus glutinosa | Alder | seed | | + | + | - | - | + |
| Quercus robur | Oak | leaf | | - | + | - | - | - |
| Quercus sp. | Oak | wood | | ++ | - | - | - | - |
| Quercus ilex | Evergreen Oak, Holm Oak | leaf | | - | + | - | - | - |

Continued

*Table 7. The waterlogged plant remains continued*

| Populus canescens | Grey Poplar | leaf | - | + | - | - | - |
|---|---|---|---|---|---|---|---|
| Salix sp. | Willow | bud | - | ++ | - | + | ++ |
| Salix sp. | Willow | capsule | - | ++ | - | - | ++ |
| Solanum sp. | Nightshade | seed | + | + | - | - | - |
| Labiatae | | seed | + | + | - | - | - |
| Lycopus europaeus | Gypsywort | seed | - | + | - | - | - |
| Prunella vulgaris | Selfheal | seed | - | + | - | - | - |
| Stachys sp. | Woundwort | seed | + | + | - | - | - |
| Lamium sp. | Dead-nettle | seed | - | + | - | - | - |
| Galeopsis sp. | Hemp-nettle | seed | - | - | - | + | - |
| cf. Marrubium vulgare | White Horehound | seed | - | + | - | - | - |
| Sambucus nigra | Elder | seed | + | + | - | - | + |
| Valerianella dentata | Narrow-fruited Cornsalad | seed | - | - | + | - | - |
| Anthemis cotula | Stinking Mayweed | seed | - | - | + | + | - |
| Arctium sp. | Burdock | seed | - | - | - | - | +++ |
| Centaurea sp. | Knapweed/Cornflower | seed | - | + | - | - | - |
| Lapsana communis | Nipplewort | seed | - | - | + | + | + |
| Picris hieracioides | Hawkweed Ox-tongue | seed | - | - | - | + | - |
| Sonchus asper | Spiny Milk-/ Sow-Thistle | seed | - | - | - | + | + |
| Juncus sp. | Rush | seed | - | - | + | - | - |
| Sparganium erectum | Branched Bur-reed | seed | + | - | - | + | - |
| Eleocharis palustris | Common Spike-rush | seed | - | + | + | + | - |
| Carex spp. | Sedges | seed | - | + | + | + | ++ |
| Lemna sp. | Duckweed | seed | ++ | ++ | + | ++ | ++ |

*sp.* suggest marshy or wet conditions adjacent to the ditches. Ruderal habitats are suggested by, for example, seeds of *Urtica dioica, Solanum sp.* (nightshade), *Pastinaca sativa* (wild parsnip), *Sambucus nigra* (elderberry) and *Chenopodium album*. So in both cases, stagnant water-filled ditches are suggested with marshy land adjacent and ruderal habitats.

Sample 108 is rather different in that it produced several leaves and buds of trees and shrubs, which suggest deliberate garden planting. Included in this group are introduced species such as *Quercus ilex* (evergreen oak), *Populus canescens* (grey poplar) and another tree identified on the basis of its small, five lobed, palmate leaf as *Aceraceae/Vitaceae* type (maple, virginia creeper etc). *Quercus ilex* has been cultivated in England since the 16th century (Bean 1914, p.311). While it may have been introduced earlier its presence with the other introduced species, particularly the *Aceraceae/Vitaceae* leaf, must suggest a late- or even post-medieval date for this feature. Of the native trees, *Sorbus aria* (white beam) grows on chalk or limestone in the wild, which suggests it must have been deliberately planted on the circum-neutral river gravels. *Quercus robus* (oak), represented by leaves, and *Salix sp.* (willow), of which there were numerous capsules and seeds, would also make impressive garden trees. In addition to the trees, seeds of *Lemna sp.* again suggest open stagnant water. Various species may have been growing on the banks of the stream or ditch such as *Brassica rapa* subsp. *sylvestris, Ranunculus sceleratus, Polygonum persicaria/*

*lapathifolium, Conium maculatum* and *Lycopus europeaus*, or on damp, marshy grounds such as *Eleocharis palustris, Ranunculus sardous* and *Potentilla anserina*. *Ranunculus bulbosus* (bulbous buttercup) and *Prunella vulgaris* (selfheal) suggest drier grassland. The remaining species are all of cultivated or ruderal habitats. The absence of truly arable weeds might suggest that they derive from settlement or, given the presence of the trees, garden habitats. Some suggestion of light soils is provided by *Chenopodium murale* (nettle-leaved goosefoot) and *Urtica urens* (small nettle).

The charred remains in samples 108 and 113 are again dominated by cereals. Sample 108 produced equal numbers of grain and rachis of free-threshing wheat, with some basal rachis of indeterminate wheat also present. Rachis of *Secale cereale* and occasionally also of *Hordeum vulgare* were also present with some grain of *Hordeum vulgare* and *Avena sp*. The same range of species was represented in sample 113 but in smaller numbers. Both samples produced occasional pulses and as with the other samples, weeds were scarce and mostly large seeded.

*Discussion*

All the samples attest to the presence of stagnant water in the ditches and pits, with no evidence of fresh flowing water. Marshy ground and possibly grassland seems to surround the features. Nitrogen rich ruderal habitats are also represented with some possible arable waste in

*Table 8. The charred plant remains*

| Latin/Scientific name | Common name | Sample | 108 | 110 | 111 | 112 | 113 |
|---|---|---|---|---|---|---|---|
| | | Context | 1337 | 1390 | 1394 | 1434 | 1481 |
| | | Feature | 1530 | 1388 | 1393 | 1067 | 1530 |
| | | Feature Type | Slot | Pit | Pit | Ditch | Ditch |
| | | Phase | 1 | 1 | 1 | 1 | 1 |
| **Cereal Remains** | | | | | | | |
| | | | | | | | |
| *Triticum sp. naked* | Free-threshing Wheat | grain | 50 | 300 | 50 | - | 10 |
| *Hordeum vulgare* | Barley | grain | 20 | 200 | 150 | - | 8 |
| *Hordeum vulgare* | Barley | rachis | 5 | 5 | 15 | - | - |
| *Secale cereale* | Rye | grain | - | - | - | - | 7 |
| *cf. Secale cereale* | cf. Rye | grain | - | - | 5 | - | - |
| *Avena sp.* | Oat | grain | 10 | 50 | 5 | - | 1 |
| *Cerealia indet* | Indeterminate cereal | grain | - | - | 50 | 1 | 9 |
| | | | | | | | |
| **Cereal Chaff** | | | | | | | |
| | | | | | | | |
| *Triticum aestivum type* | Bread Type Wheat | rachis | - | 20 | 5 | - | 2 |
| *Triticum sp. naked* | Free-threshing Wheat | rachis | 50 | - | 10 | - | 2 |
| *Triticum sp. naked* | Free-threshing Wheat | basal rachis | - | - | 2 | - | - |
| *Triticum sp.* | Wheat | basal rachis | 10 | - | - | - | - |
| *Secale cereale* | Rye | rachis | 10 | - | 1 | - | - |
| *Secale/Hordeum sp.* | Rye/Barley | rachis | - | 5 | 25 | - | 1 |
| *Avena sp.* | Oat | floret base | - | 1 | - | - | - |
| *Cerealia indet* | Indeterminate cereal | rachis | - | - | 5 | - | - |
| *Cerealia indet* | Indeterminate cereal | basal rachis | - | 5 | 1 | - | - |
| *Cerealia indet* | Indeterminate cereal | culm node | - | - | 5 | - | 1 |
| *Cerealia indet* | Indeterminate cereal | embryo | - | - | 2 | - | - |
| | | | | | | | |
| **Other Cultivated Species** | | | | | | | |
| | | | | | | | |
| *Vicia/Pisum sp.* | Vetch/Pea | pulse | 5 | 10 | 5 | - | 3 |
| | | | | | | | |
| **Weed Species** | | | | | | | |
| | | | | | | | |
| *Chenopodiaceae* | | seed | - | - | - | - | 1 |
| *Chenopodium album* | Fat Hen | seed | 5 | - | - | - | 2 |
| *Atriplex sp.* | Orache | seed | 2 | 10 | - | - | - |
| *Leguminosae* | | seed | - | 10 | - | - | 1 |
| *Crataegus sp.* | Hawthorn | seed | - | - | - | - | 1 |
| *Rumex sp.* | Docks | seed | 2 | 10 | - | - | - |
| *Anthemis cotula* | Stinking Mayweed | seed | - | - | - | - | 1 |
| *Eleocharis palustris* | Common Spike-rush | seed | - | 10 | 3 | - | - |
| *Carex spp.* | Sedges | seed | - | - | 1 | - | - |
| *Gramineae large* | large seeded grass | seed | - | - | 1 | | |

samples 112 and 111. Sample 108 produced an interesting range of garden tree and shrubs, although the unusual introduced species suggest that later disturbance had affected the integrity of this context.

The charred cereal remains are rich but are otherwise in keeping with rural settlements of the 12th/13th century, involved in cereal production (Grieg, 1991). The four major cereal staples are all represented: bread wheat, barley, oats and rye. Rivet wheat is not represented although it is know from other sites of this date (Moffet, 1991). Legumes are also represented. While flax is absent from the samples, the presence of weeds usually associated with it may suggest flax was being cultivated. The presence of rachis in good numbers in samples 108 and 111 might be indicative of the use of cereal straw. Indeed wheat rachis outnumbers grain in sample 108 and includes basal nodes, which is in keeping with the complete ear being utilised from which some grain has been shaken free. If straw was being used for thatching, for example, it is unlikely that the ear would be removed first. The cereal species represented would be used for a range of possible functions, including animal fodder, brewing, thatching, fuel, flour and whole grain for human consumption.

## Insects and molluscs
*by Mark Robinson*

### Introduction

Following the assessment and analysis of macroscopic plant remains, four of the same five samples were subjected to insect analysis: sample 112 from a 12th-century ditch fill, samples 108 and 113 from probable 12th/13th-century ditches or slots, and sample 111 from a probable 13th-century pit. Mollusc shells were present in sample 112, which were also analysed. Sample 107 came from a probable late medieval or post-medieval water feature (1058).

### Methods and results

Samples of 5 kg were washed over onto a 0.25 mm sieve and sorted in water under a binocular microscope for biological remains, including insects and molluscs, which were identified. The results are given in Tables 9 and 10, nomenclature following Kloet and Hincks (1977) for Coleoptera (beetles) and Kerney (1999) for Mollusca. Presence only was recorded for the Coleoptera, but no species was represented by more than two individuals in any sample. Almost all the insects were Coleoptera and other orders have not been recorded.

### Interpretation

The samples all contained somewhat similar assemblages of beetles, although poor preservation in sample 111 resulted in few of the remains being identifiable. They included water beetles which favour small bodies of stagnant water, particularly *Helophorus cf. brevipalpis*, but also *Hydrobius fuscipes*, *Anacaena globulus* and *Ochthebius sp. H. fuscipes* and *A. globulus*

often occur in pools with much detrital plant material. The molluscs from sample 112, from the 12th-century ditch (1067), included *Planorbis planorbis* and *Gyraulus albus*, which together suggested well-vegetated, stagnant or slowly flowing water. In contrast, however, sample 107 (ditch 1058) contained two examples of *Normandia nitens*, an elmid beetle which requires very clean flowing water.

Evidence for marsh and waterside vegetation was given by the occurrence of the weevil *Notaris acridulus* in several of the samples. *Prasocuris phellandrii*, a leaf beetle which feeds on aquatic *Umbelliferae*, such as *Oenanthe aquatica* (water dropwort) and *Apium nodiflorum* (fool's watercress), was identified from sample 107.

The terrestrial landscape largely seems to have been open. The weevils *Apion spp.* and *Sitona sp.* feed on various vetches and clovers. *Chaetocnema concinna*, a flea beetle which feeds on *Polygonum spp.* (knotgrass etc) and *Rumex spp.* (docks), was present in three of the samples. The grazing of domestic animals was suggested by dung beetles from the genus *Aphodius*, which were found in all but sample 111. The only evidence for trees given by the insects was provided by *Chalcoides sp.* from sample 111 and *Phyllodecta sp.* from sample 113. Both beetles feed on the leaves of *spp. Populus* (poplars) and *Salix spp.* (willows).

There was little evidence from the insects for settlement structures or activities. Single examples of *Anobium punctatum* (woodworm beetle), which particularly attacks the timbers of buildings, were found in sample 108 (context 1336) and sample 113 (context 1485), two of the probable 12th/13th-century ditches or slots. However, insects suggestive of other indoor habitats, large-scale grain storage or substantial accumulations of decaying refuse, were absent.

### Conclusions

The insects and molluscs from the various 12th/13th-century ditches, slots and pits suggest that they held water and that marsh or aquatic plants grew alongside or in them. Only from context 1053 (the fill of a late- or post-medieval garden feature) was there evidence for flowing water. The surrounding landscape seems largely to have been grazed pasture, although some poplar or willow trees perhaps grew along the water courses.

## DISCUSSION

The scope for interpretation of the results for Poyle House is limited. Extensive landscaping and levelling in the past had removed much of the medieval and early post-medieval remains from the area seen in plan, and very few finds were recovered. A more complete stratigraphic sequence survived to the south of the excavations, but this area was note excavated and has been preserved *in situ*. Consequently, the best stratigraphic sequences have been seen in section only, offering little scope for interpretation of the nature or extent of the structures or occupation they represent.

*Table 9. Coleoptera*

| Latin/Scientific name | Sample | 107 | 108 | 111 | 112 | 113 |
|---|---|---|---|---|---|---|
| | Context | 1093 | 1337 | 1394 | 1434 | 1481 |
| | Feature | 1058 | 1530 | 1393 | 1067 | 1530 |
| | Sample Weight (kg) | 5 | 5 | 5 | 5 | 5 |
| *Carabus* sp. | | - | - | - | - | + |
| *Nebria brevicollis* (F.) | | - | + | - | - | + |
| *Trechus obtusus* Er. or *quadristriatus* (Schr.) | | - | + | - | - | - |
| *Bembidion* sp. | | - | - | - | + | + |
| *Pterostichus melanarius* (Ill.) | | - | - | - | - | + |
| *P. cupreus* (L.) *or versicolor* (Sturm) | | - | - | - | - | + |
| *Agonum* sp. | | - | - | - | - | + |
| *Helophorus aquaticus* (L.) *or grandis* Ill. | | - | - | - | - | + |
| *Helophorus* spp. (*brevipalpis size*) | | + | + | - | + | + |
| *Cercyon* sp. | | - | - | + | - | + |
| *Megasternum obscurum* (Marsh.) | | - | + | - | - | - |
| *Hydrobius fuscipes* (L.) | | + | - | - | + | + |
| *Anacaena globulus* (Pk.) | | - | - | - | - | + |
| *Ochthebius* sp. | | - | - | + | + | - |
| *Hydraena* sp. | | - | - | - | - | + |
| *Choleva* or *Catops* sp. | | - | + | - | - | + |
| *Omalium* sp. | | - | - | - | - | + |
| *Lesteva longoelytrata* (Gz.) | | - | - | - | - | + |
| *Coprophilus striatulus* (F.) | | - | - | - | - | + |
| *Anotylus rugosus* (F.) | | + | + | - | - | + |
| *Lathrobium* sp. (not *longulum*) | | - | + | - | - | + |
| *Rugilus* sp. | | - | - | - | - | + |
| *Philonthus* spp. | | - | - | - | - | + |
| *Aphodius granarius* (L.) | | - | - | - | - | + |
| *A. cf. sphacelatus* (Pz.) | | - | + | - | - | + |
| *Aphodius* spp. | | + | - | - | + | + |
| *Oxyomus sylvestris* (Scop.) | | - | - | - | - | + |
| *Normandia nitens* (Müll.) | | + | - | - | - | - |
| *Anobium punctatum* (F.) | | - | + | - | - | + |
| *Meligethes* sp. | | - | - | - | - | + |
| Cryptophagidae indet. (not Atomaria) | | - | - | - | - | + |
| *Atomaria sp.* | | - | + | - | - | - |
| *Lathridius minutus* gp. | | - | + | - | - | - |
| *Chrysolina* sp. | | - | - | - | - | + |
| *Phyllodecta* sp. | | - | - | - | - | + |
| *Prasocuris phellandrii* (L.) | | + | - | - | - | - |
| *Longitarsus* spp. | | - | - | - | + | - |
| *Chalcoides* sp. | | - | - | + | - | - |
| *Chaetocnema concinna* (Marsh.) | | - | + | - | + | + |
| *Apion* spp. | | + | - | - | + | + |
| *Phyllobius* sp. | | - | - | - | + | - |
| *Sitona* sp. | | - | - | - | + | - |
| *Hypera* sp. (not *punctata*) | | + | - | - | - | - |
| *Notaris acridulus* (L.) | | - | + | + | | |
| Ceuthorhynchinae indet. | | - | - | - | - | + |

*Table 10. Mollusca*

| | Sample | 112 |
|---|---|---|
| | Context | 1434 |
| | Feature | 1433 |
| | Sample Weight (kg) | 5 |
| *Lymnaea sp.* | | 1 |
| *Planorbis planorbis* (L.) | | 9 |
| *Anisus vortex* (L.) | | 7 |
| *Gyraulus crista* (L.) | | 1 |

A number of conclusions can be reached with reasonable confidence, particularly regarding the earlier chronology and the sequence of development of the site, and these are presented below.

**Pre-medieval activity**

The small flint assemblage (see Lamdin-Whymark) and the two residual Romano-British sherds point to a very low level of activity prior to the 11th century. It might be supposed that the low-lying marshy environment would not have made this area a focus for occupation until population pressure or the slow trend towards a drier climate towards the turn of the 1st millennium AD alleviated conditions on the site.

**The structural development of the medieval farm 12th-17th centuries (Figure 7)**

The pottery suggests that the site was first occupied towards the end of the 11th century, which tallies well with the first mention of the manor at Stanwell in Domesday. Although it cannot be stated categorically that this site represents part of the subsidiary estate mentioned in Domesday, the archaeological evidence points to the existence of at least two buildings, likely to be elements of a farming settlement dating to the 12th century. The suggestion of status in the animal bone assemblage may indicate something wealthier than a peasant holding.

The two buildings of the first phase appeared to be separated by a cluster of postholes, possibly defining a gateway. The northern building, partially revealed in plan, may have been a barn, as suggested by the presence of large quantities of cereal grain in the beamslots and adjacent pits. The southern building, whose north wall was probably situated just north of the south baulk of the excavation, appears to have been constructed on a platform of silty clay, presumably to ensure a drier internal environment. The proximity of the water table to the medieval ground surface is indicated by the environmental samples, which show that there would have been standing water in the ditches for long periods each year. Further proof of the damp environment is provided by the survival of three pieces of worked wood in the ditch fills. Little need be added to Mitchell's analysis of the post fragment and barrel end. The possible wheel felloe appears to be an element of some mechanical device, and is in some ways

characteristic of a mill gearwheel, although there are serious doubts generated by the physical characteristics of the wheel. Furthermore, no other archaeological, historical or topographical evidence was found to support the contention that a mill was ever sited here. The mill mentioned as part of the Poyle estate is (as suggested above) most likely to be the one situated to the east in Poyle village itself. In conclusion therefore, while the felloe appears to be part of a mechanical device, and possibly one employed to raise water, it is most unlikely to be part of a mill gearwheel.

The size or groundplan of the 12th - to 13th-century house is difficult to estimate. From the limited archaeological evidence one may hypothesise an original rectangular building, approximately 6 m wide. On the basis of evidence from elsewhere, the house could have been around 12 m long, and probably divided into bays. Examples of similar houses, representing farmhouses of reasonable, if not particularly elevated status, can be found across lowland England. The 12th-13th-century manor at Wintringham, Huntingdonshire, had a simple rectangular hall with internal subdivisions (Hurst 1988, 871 and fig. 9.6), and may be comparable with the building at Poyle.

There is some indication of an expansion or redevelopment of the farm in the late medieval or early post-medieval period. The presence of early bricks, either in fragmentary form in demolition layers, or apparently reused in more modern footings, suggests that the original building may have been enlarged. Brick nogging, or the replacement of wattle and daub infilling of the timber frame with brickwork, is not thought to have been common until the late 16th century (Wood 1965, 225). The sequence of floor layers and a tiled hearth in the southern section point to the continued occupation of the house, and, if the hypothetical north wall was in the same position, the presence of the hearth suggests that a chimney stack was at some stage inserted into the wall.

Other indications of further development of the farm include the possible outbuilding revealed in the eastern part of the trench by features 1015, 1352 and 1353 and the posthole group 1236. The absence of late medieval finds from the boundary ditches suggests that these had been filled in (or had silted up gradually). To the west of the house another outbuilding is suggested by the two possible beamslots 1156 and 1170, and the intervening gravel floor surface.

The dearth of finds dating from later than the 12th and 13th centuries cannot be taken at face value to suggest an absence of occupation. The documentary sources clearly point to a flourishing and developing establishment. Given the development of the farm around a courtyard, it is reasonable to expect that rubbish would be disposed of outside that central area (and beyond the excavation site). The truncation of the area undertaken prior to the construction of the new house would have removed any material that had accumulated.

It can therefore be concluded that, despite the limitations of the surviving archaeological record, there

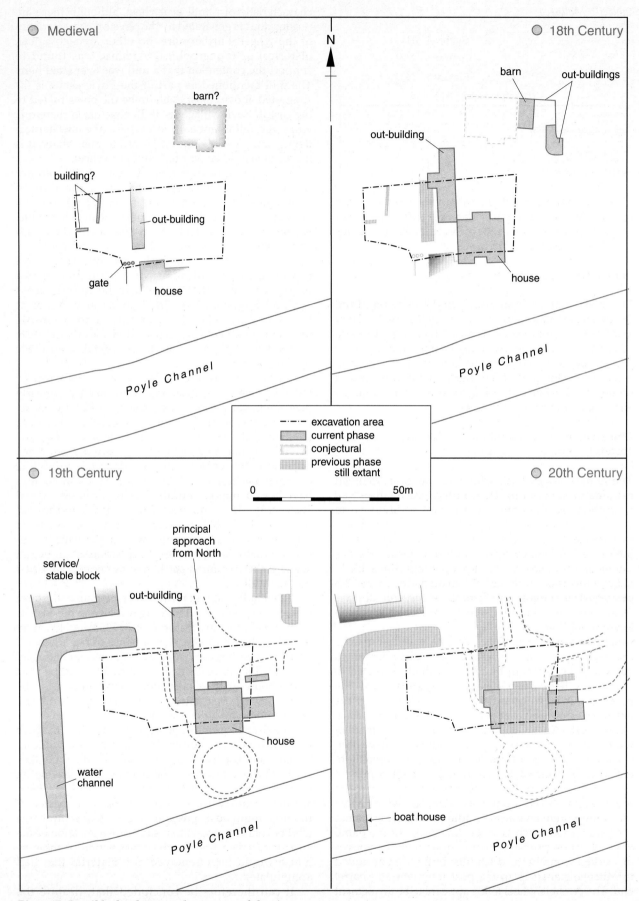

*Figure 7. Possible developmental sequence of the site.*

appeared to be a thriving and developing farm on the site with extensive arable and pastoral interests during the late medieval and early post medieval periods, a contention that is supported by the historical evidence.

## The 18th-century rebuilding

The historical record and the RCHME inspection carried out in 1936 indicate that early in the 18th century a new house was constructed. Significantly, the archaeological evidence indicates that the new house footprint lay immediately to the east of the old house, which might suggest that the old house (or part of it) still stood, at least during the construction of the new building. On the face of it, this appears to put in doubt any possibility that some elements of the old house may have been incorporated into the new one *in situ*, although, as the survey suggested, it is quite possible that the fireplace could have been dismantled and rebuilt, and salvaged bricks incorporated into the new building.

However, although no evidence was recovered from the excavation to indicate as much, it is highly likely that the original, almost certainly rectangular house was enlarged, possibly with a cross wing extending to the east, so that the final medieval version of the house may well have extended under the footprint of the later house, but only the projecting west wing (the original part of the house) would have been exposed in the excavation. Thus the facade of the medieval house may well ultimately have been to the north. By the 16th century there was a widespread belief in the efficacy of facing a house to the north or north-east, providing shelter from the south and south-west wind. As a contemporary self-appointed authority on health, Andrew Boorde avowed "the south wind doth corrupt and make for evil vapours", while the east wind was "temperate, fryske and fragraunt" (Cook 1974, 43).

The decision to remove only the northern wall of the medieval house, while apparently leaving the rest intact, is curious, but could be seen as support for the hypothesis that the erstwhile timber-framed house had - by the 17th century - a brick chimney stack incorporated into the north wall. Removal of the north wall would have provided a considerable quantity of reusable bricks.

Although construction of the new house avoided the footprint of at least part of the old one, the decision was taken to clear away all the material from the yard to the north of the house. The survey map of 1748 (see front cover) shows the new house facing north onto a yard, with what appears to be a barn opposite, and a long range immediately to the west. The brick footings of this range were located in plan and section during the excavation, and again they are situated immediately to the east of the footprint of the earlier west range.

The apparent continuity of the conjunction of these two buildings suggests that the arrangement of the principal farm buildings around a central courtyard may have been established well before the building of the new house. The plan of the large building opposite the house in the 1748 map is characteristic of a medieval barn, with a projecting wagon porch. The fact that its alignment does not match that of the Georgian house could also be construed as support for this hypothesis.

The 1738 survey map depicts a complex of buildings clustered round a courtyard. It could be argued that the map shows the estate in transition from a working, prosperous farm to a gentrified country residence. The new house can be seen as a modest manifestation of the new Palladian style, but instead of an immense sprawling facade, the wings of the house were effectively folded back, resulting in an approximately square plan. It has been suggested that 'the wings-folded' arrangement worked very well for houses built for 'people of moderate fortunes but sophisticated tastes' (Girouard 1978, 160). To the west, south and east of the house are gardens and orchards, reflecting a growing fashion in the 17th and 18th centuries for decorative landscapes. To the north of the complex, however, the names of the fields - 'Great Tar Close', 'Little Tar Close', 'Glue Yard' 'Lime Yard' are perhaps a legacy of a much more utilitarian, almost industrial environment in the recent past, and perhaps reflect the subordinate nature of the relationship between Poyle House and Stanwell Manor in the 17th century.

The OS Map of 1866 shows that by the mid 19th century the emphasis had shifted away from the practicalities of a working farm and towards a more fashionable landscaped setting for a country house. The 'farmyard' had gone, exposing the north front of the house to view from the new approach along the drive running south from the lodge on the Bath Road. The gardens to the west of the house were now augmented with a decorative 'moat' or water channel, to the north of which was situated the servants' quarters, stables and other service rooms grouped around their own courtyard. No evidence was found during the excavation to suggest that this channel ever fully encircled the house. Not only was there no indication of a moat on the 1748 map, but the presence of a fully developed moat, even approximately following the line of the 19th-century feature, would have required a very different layout of the farm courtyard, and this would surely have been reflected in the layout of buildings depicted.

The final major changes in this 'gentrification' of the environs of Poyle House are apparent in the 1896 OS map which show the disappearance of the attached west range, leaving the house standing separate from other buildings, and the revival of the approach to the house from Poyle village to the east.

A few of the features (other than the main walls) relating to the layout of the 18th-century house, or later developments within it, were identified in the excavation. These included four soakaways, close to the eastern edge of the trench, which would have been situated in the east wing. This wing does not appear on the 1748 map, but is present on the OS map of 1866, and is enlarged to the east and north thereafter. Given that apparently re-used Tudor brickwork was noted in the south front of this wing in the 1936 survey, it is likely that it was constructed by the mid-18th century. Also noted in the east baulk section was the remains of a brick floor, with a central gutter or drain, support for the likelihood of the wing originally being the service wing to the house.

## Acknowledgments

The excavation and subsequent report were funded by Gulf Air, whose help and co-operation throughout the project is gratefully acknowledged. Special thanks are due to Douglas Norwood, the Project Manager. The authors would like to thank Stephen Naylor of Hampshire County Council Planning Department (Archaeology and Historic Buildings) for his advice and suggestions regarding the wheel felloe. The drawing of the wheel felloe is by Leslie Collet; all other illustrations are by Sarah Lucas. The text was edited by Anne Dodd and typeset by Steven Cheshire.

# BIBLIOGRAPHY

Bean, WJ, 1914 *Trees and shrubs hardy in the British Isles,* **Vol 2l**, London

Boessneck, J, 1969 Osteological Differences in Sheep (*Ovis aries Linné*) and Goat (*Capra hircus Linné*), in D Brothwell and E Higgs (eds) *Science in Archaeology,* London

Brunskill, RW, 1990 *Brick Building in Britain,* London

Clapham, AR, Tutin, TG, and Moore, M, 1989 *Flora of the British Isles,* 3rd ed., Cambridge

Cook, O, 1974 *The English Country House,* London

Crossley, D, 1975 *Bewl Valley Ironworks, Kent,* c1300-1730, Royal Archaeological Institute Monograph, London

Girouard, M, 1978 *Life in the English Country House,* London

Greig, JRA, 1991 *The British Isles,* in W Van Zeist, K Wasylikowa and K-E Behre (eds) *Progress in Old World Palaeoethnobotany,* Rotterdam.

Hinton, DA, 1974 'M.40 Ware' in DA Hinton and T Rowley, *Excavations on the Route of the M.40,* Oxford

Hurst, JG, 1988 'Rural building in England' in J Thirsk (ed) *The Agrarian History of England and Wales* **Vol II,** 1042-1350, Cambridge

Kerney, MP, 1999 *Atlas of the land and freshwater molluscs of Britain and Ireland,* Colchester

Kloet, GS, and Hincks W D, 1977 *A check list of British insects, 2nd edition (revised): Coleoptera and Strepsiptera,* Royal Entomological Society of London; Handbook for the Identification of British Insects 11, pt 3, London

Lyman, RL, 1996, *Vertebrate Taphonomy.* Cambridge Manuals in Archaeology, Cambridge

McCarthy, MR, and Brooks, CM, 1988 *Medieval Pottery in Britain AD900-1600,* Leicester

Mellor, M, 1994 'Oxford Pottery: A Synthesis of middle and late Saxon, medieval and early post-medieval pottery in the Oxford Region', *Oxoniensia* **59**

Moffett, L, 1991 The Archaeobotanical Evidence for Free-Threshing Tetraploid Wheat in Britain, in E. Hajnalova (ed) *Palaeoethnobotany and Archaeology,* IWGP 8th Symposium, Acta Interdisciplinaria Archaeologica, Tomus **VII**, Nitra

Pike, G, 1965 A Medieval Pottery Kiln site on the Camley Gardens Estate, Maidenhead *Berks Archaeol J,* **62**

Payne, S, 1973 Kill-off patterns in Sheep and Goats: The Mandibles from Asvan Kale. *Anatolian Studies* **23**

Prummel, W, and Frisch, H-J, 1986 A Guide for the distinction of species, sex and body size in bones of sheep and goat. *Journal of Archaeological Science,* **XIII**

Reynolds, TS, 1985 Clasp arms versus compass arms in water wheels, in E Hook and R Palsson, (eds) 1985 *Medieval iron in society,* Jernkontoret and Riksantikvarieambetet, Jernkontorets Forskning **H34**

Salisbury, C, 1995 The excavation of Hemington Fields, *Current Archaeology* **145**

Silver, IA, 1969 'The Ageing of Domestic Animals' in D Brothwell & E Higgs, (eds) *Science in Archaeology,* London

Smith, PT, 1999 Assessment of the Bricks from The Oracle Site, Reading, Berkshire, Phase II Post Excavation Assessment. Oxford Archaeological Unit

VCH: Victoria County History of Middlesex, **III** (1962), London

Vince, AG, 1985 The Saxon and Medieval Pottery of London: A review, *Medieval Archaeology* **29**

von den Driesch, A, 1976 *A Guide to the Measurement of Animal Bones from Archaeological Sites,* Peabody Museum Bulletin 1, Peabody Museum of Archaeology and Ethnology, Harvard University

Wilkinson, D (ed.) 1992 The Oxford Archaeological Unit Field Manual

Wood, M, 1965 *The English Medieval House,* London

# APPENDIX 1

*Pottery occurence by number and weight (in g) of sherds per context by fabric type.*

| | RB | | ESUR | | 300 | | 360 | | EMSH | | CAMG | | SHER | | SAND | | LOND | | CBW | | BRILL | | TUDG | | RE | | |
|---|---|---|---|---|---|---|---|---|---|---|---|---|---|---|---|---|---|---|---|---|---|---|---|---|---|---|---|
| | No | Wt | No | Wt | No | Wt | No | Wt | No | Wt | No | Wt | No | Wt | No | Wt | No | Wt | No | Wt | No | Wt | No | Wt | No | Wt | DATE |
| 1021 | | | | | | | | | | | | | | | | | | | 1 | 61 | | | | | | | L13thC |
| 1025 | | | 2 | 63 | | | 1 | 14 | 2 | 24 | 8 | 245 | | | | | | | | | | | | | | | 12thC |
| 1035 | | | | | | | | | | | | | | | | | | | 1 | 69 | | | | | | | L13thC |
| 1054 | | | | | | | | | | | | | 1 | 2 | 1 | 15 | | | | | | | | | | | 12thC |
| 1055 | | | | | | | | | 1 | 5 | | | 2 | 19 | | | | | | | | | | | | | 12thC |
| 1057 | | | | | | | | | 1 | 15 | | | | | | | | | | | | | | | | | 11th-12thC |
| 1061 | | | 1 | 8 | 1 | 14 | | | | | | | 1 | 6 | | | | | | | | | | | | | 12thC? |
| 1065 | | | | | | | | | | | 1 | 12 | | | | | | | | | | | | | | | 12thC? |
| 1094 | | | | | | | | | | | | | 2 | 236 | | | | | | | | | | | | | 12thC |
| 1153 | | | | | | | 1 | 9 | | | 1 | 9 | | | | | | | | | | | | | | | 12thC? |
| 1176 | | | | | | | 1 | 28 | | | 1 | 26 | | | | | | | | | | | | | | | 12thC |
| 1181 | | | 1 | 5 | | | | | | | | | | | | | | | | | | | | | | | 11th-12thC |
| 1208 | | | | | 2 | 47 | | | | | | | | | | | | | | | | | | | | | 12thC? |
| 1216 | | | | | | | | | | | 3 | 50 | | | | | | | | | | | | | | | 12thC |
| 1299 | | | | | | | | | | | 1 | 2 | | | | | | | | | | | | | | | 12thC? |
| 1313 | 1 | 11 | | | | | | | | | | | | | | | | | | | | | | | | | RB?? |
| 1315 | | | | | | | 3 | 52 | 7 | 236 | 6 | 125 | 4 | 106 | 4 | 164 | 1 | 3 | | | | | | | | | 12thC |
| 1318 | | | | | | | | | | | 1 | 26 | | | | | | | | | | | | | | | 12thC? |
| 1326 | 1 | 17 | | | | | | | | | | | | | | | | | | | | | | | | | RB?? |
| 1328 | | | 1 | 4 | | | | | | | | | | | | | | | | | | | | | | | 11th-12thC |
| 1344 | | | | | | | | | 2 | 13 | | | 1 | 3 | | | | | | | | | | | | | 12thC? |
| 1390 | | | | | | | | | 1 | 36 | | | 7 | 314 | | | | | | | | | | | | | 12thC |
| 1391 | | | | | | | | | 1 | 34 | 1 | 41 | 2 | 45 | | | | | | | | | | | | | 12thC |
| 1395 | | | 1 | 14 | | | | | | | | | | | | | | | | | | | | | | | 11th-12thC |
| 1396 | | | 2 | 17 | | | | | 5 | 108 | | | | | | | | | | | | | | | | | 11th-12thC |
| 1403 | 1 | 1 | | | | | | | | | 1 | 18 | | | | | | | | | | | | | | | 12thC? |
| 1415 | | | | | | | | | | | | | | | | | | | | | | | 1 | 5 | 2 | 76 | 16thC |
| 1481 | | | | | | | | | | | | | | | | | | | | | 1 | 71 | | | | | 14thC |
| 1486 | | | | | 2 | 23 | | | | | | | 1 | 73 | | | | | 3 | 59 | | | | | | | L13thC |
| 1540 | | | | | 4 | 322 | | | 1 | 8 | | | | | | | | | 1 | 57 | | | | | | | L13thC |
| 1543 | | | | | | | | | | | | | 2 | 8 | | | | | | | | | | | | | 12thC? |
| 1551 | | | 1 | 25 | | | | | | | 1 | 25 | | | | | | | | | | | | | | | 12thC? |
| 1552 | | | | | | | 1 | 6 | | | | | | | | | | | | | | | | | | | 12thC? |
| 1555 | | | | | | | 1 | 36 | | | 2 | 7 | | | | | | | | | | | | | | | 13thC? |
| 1565 | | | | | 2 | 81 | | | | | | | | | | | | | | | | | | | | | 12thC? |
| 1566 | | | 1 | 9 | 5 | 638 | | | 1 | 6 | 2 | 54 | 3 | 68 | | | | | | | | | | | | | 12thC |
| 1575 | | | | | 1 | 21 | | | | | | | | | | | | | | | | | | | | | 12thC? |
| 1577 | | | 1 | 28 | | | | | | | | | | | | | | | | | | | | | | | 11th-12thC |
| 1581 | | | | | | | | | 1 | 4 | | | | | | | | | | | | | | | | | 11th-12thC |
| 1583 | | | | | | | | | | | 1 | 33 | | | | | | | | | | | | | | | 12thC? |
| 1585 | | | | | | | 1 | 8 | | | | | | | | | | | | | | | | | | | 12thC? |
| | 3 | 29 | 11 | 173 | 17 | 1146 | 9 | 153 | 23 | 489 | 32 | 681 | 24 | 872 | 5 | 179 | 1 | 3 | 6 | 246 | 1 | 71 | 1 | 5 | 2 | 76 | |

## APPENDIX 2

*Measurements of animal bones by phase, species and element after von den Driesch (1976)*

| Phase | Species | Element | GL | Bp | Bfp | SD | BD | Dd |
|---|---|---|---|---|---|---|---|---|
| 1 | Horse | Radius | 315 | 71 | 64.7 | 31 | 65.8 | |
| 1 | Cat | Tibia | | | | | 9.8 | |
| 2 | Cattle | Metatarsal | 181 | 49 | | 34.5 | 49.9 | |
| 2 | Horse | Metatarsal | 245.5 | 43 | | 26.7 | 44.5 | |
| 2 | Horse | Metacarpal | 225 | 43.1 | | 27 | 44.4 | |
| | | | GLC | Bp | Bfp | SD | BD | Dd |
| 2 | Dog | Femur | 184.5 | | | 10.5 | 28.5 | 35 |
| 2 | Dog | Femur | 184.5 | 36 | | 10.5 | 28 | 31 |